SCANT HOURS

SCANT HOURS

SELECTED POEMS OF
ELISABETH SCHMEIDEL

TRANSLATED BY
STUART FRIEBERT

PINYON PUBLISHING
Montrose, Colorado

ALSO BY ELISABETH SCHMEIDEL

Stirngewächse herzverwurzelt (poems in the original German
published by scaneg Verlag/Munich)

ALSO BY STUART FRIEBERT

PROSE
First and Last Words: Memoir & Stories
Der Gast, und sei er noch so schlecht: Prose Sketches
The Language of the Enemy: Stories

POETRY
Dreaming of Floods

Calming Down

Up in Bed

Stories My Father Can Tell

Uncertain Health

The Darmstadt Orchids

Funeral Pie

Near Occasions of Sin

Speak Mouth to Mouth

Floating Heart

On the Bottom

Decanting: Selected & New Poems

Kein Trinkwasser

Die Prokuristen kommen

Nicht Hinauslehnen

ANTHOLOGIES

A Field Guide to Contemporary Poetry & Poetics
  (with David Young; Second edition with David Walker and David Young)

The Longman Anthology of Contemporary American Poetry
  (First and Second editions: with David Young)

Models of the Universe: An Anthology of the Prose Poem
  (with David Young)

TRANSLATIONS

Günter Eich: Valuable Nail: Selected Poems
  (with David Walker and David Young)

Karl Krolow: On Account Of: Selected Poems

Miroslav Holub: Sagittal Section: Selected Poems
  (with Dana Habová)

Giovanni Raboni: The Coldest Year of Grace: Selected Poems
  (with Vinio Rossi)

Marin Sorescu: Hands Behind My Back: Selected Poems
  (with Gabriela Dragnea and Adriana Varga)

Karl Krolow: What'll We Do With This Life?: Selected Poems

Judita Vaičiūnaitė: Fire, Put Out By Fire: Selected Poems
  (with Viktoria Skrupskelis)

Sylva Fischerová: The Swing in the Middle of Chaos: Selected Poems
  (with the author)

Sylva Fischerová: Stomach of the Soul: Selected Poems
  (with the author and A. J. Hauner)

Karl Krolow: Puppets in the Wind: Selected Poems

Kuno Raeber: Be Quiet: Selected Poems

Kuno Raeber: Watch Out: Selected Poems

Kuno Raeber: Votives: Selected Poems
  (with Christiane Wyrwa)

TEXTBOOK

Max Frisch: Als der Krieg zu Ende war

Cover and Interior Art by Elisabeth Schmeidel

Photographs of Elisabeth Schmeidel by Pia Grubbauer

Photograph of Stuart Friebert by Cynthia Sanders

Design by Susan Entsminger

First Edition: March 2018

Pinyon Publishing
23847 V66 Trail, Montrose, CO 81403
www.pinyon-publishing.com

Library of Congress Control Number: 2018934035
ISBN: 978-1-936671-49-6

ACKNOWLEDGMENTS

This collection owes a great deal to Elisabeth Schmeidel's daughter, Pia Grubbauer, for permission to publish the poems and for a number of helpful suggestions.

Thanks to scaneg Verlag/Munich, which has published *Stirngewächse herzverwurzelt*, the German originals, for its support.

Thanks to Thomas Wild for carefully reviewing the translations, as well as his introduction.

Special thanks to Susan & Gary Entsminger for helpful, incisive comments & suggestions all along, as well as Susan's designing gifts.

Finally, thanks to the editors of the following journals in which some of the poems have previously appeared, sometimes in slightly different form: *Bangalore Review, Bitter Oleander, Copper Nickel, Field, OffCourse, Osiris, Pinyon Review, The Red Wheelbarrow, Solstice*, and *Voyages*.

IN MEMORY

of

ELISABETH SCHMEIDEL / 1945–2012

R.I.P.

CONTENTS

II LATER

III LATER STILL

INTRODUCTION

By Thomas Wild

This volume offers a chance for discovery: of poems and a poet. Yet really, they should already be well known to us. We ought to be as familiar with Elisabeth Schmeidel as we are with her canonized colleagues Paul Celan, Ingeborg Bachmann, Günter Eich, Ilse Aichinger, Jürgen Becker, and Nicholas Born. Ought to be, if it depended only on the texts and the power of the language. But it is often simply luck, good or bad, that decides who is remembered, who becomes inscribed in the literary memory of a certain time. Regardless of whose will it was that Elisabeth Schmeidel's poems never appeared in book form during her lifetime, it is unquestionably a stroke of luck that we now have this marvelous collection, selected by Stuart Friebert with Schmeidel's daughter, Pia Grubbauer, and translated by Friebert into English. The subtle and thoughtful composition of *Scant Hours* guides us through Schmeidel's *early, later,* and *later still* poetic worlds. Suddenly, we find ourselves on a true voyage of discovery.

The *EARLY* world is marked by time. "On one day," begins one poem; "Late afternoon in November," begins another. Schmeidel gives dates, the circumstances of her writing. She roots her writing in a here and now, and takes note of it. A poem titled "Daily Memo" ends with the line "a gang of guards takes charge of the graves of heroes." It is an injured time that we encounter in these poems—a time marked by war, by violence, by fear, by "submarine mines," and a "many-thousand-year Reich." Writing requires one to be mindful of one's dates, Paul Celan once said, meaning one's personal and political circumstances. The crucial date for Schmeidel was 1945, the year of her birth. Her writing remained mindful of that date, most explicitly in the early years.

In encountering the decades after the Second World War through the eyes and ears, images and sounds of Elisabeth

Schmeidel's poems, we see the urgent tasks of this first post-war generation: to look closely, to take notice and take notes, to weigh words, soft and sharp, to take off one's armor and allow the skin to sense—above all to sense the individual's relationship to "time," or rather to the complex layering of times and pasts: "On one day / […] the sun, rising, / will break through / the skin of the earth and / […] as usual / you'll / do everything normally / while the ground / under your feet / burns" ("Instructions"). The "you" (plural, in the German) in Schmeidel's poems is the subject sometimes of appeal, sometimes of accusation. The distance between speaker and addressees lends a particular urgency to the lyric voice.

In Schmeidel's tone, themes, and vocabulary there are echoes of writers from the same time period. Her subtle and shrewd mind responded in its own way to what was "in the air" at the time. And certainly, art is born not least of all from art. And so repeated motifs of time, memory, mysterious flowers, layering (in "Geological," for instance), and words like ashes, rubble, dark, or eye find poetic resonance with the work of Paul Celan. Schmeidel's fondness for lyric lists, on the one hand, and her play with the motif of advice and affinity for "snow" and "winter" (see "A Year Before," "This Winter"), on the other, are reminiscent respectively of Günter Eich and Ilse Aichinger (Stuart Friebert writes of Schmeidel's encounter with the latter in his afterword). Above all, one senses a conversation with Ingeborg Bachmann. Schmeidel's "Observation," "This Winter," "Geological," and "Scant Hours" share a fundamental vocabulary and subtle overtones with her Austrian colleague. Schmeidel's constellation of pivotal motifs—fog, midday, autumn, shadows, dream, collapse, diving—is hard to imagine without an encounter with Bachmann's poems from *Die gestundete Zeit* and *Anrufung des großen Bären*, as can be seen, for example, when one compares the famous title poem from the former volume with Schmeidel's "One Last Time": "Set loose your anchors from this house / now and not a day later. // For the last time doves / cry over the breakers, hunt / fish back to the sea." Knowing that it was too late for "silent mourning," Schmeidel shares with these other authors the challenge of exploring the possibilities of mindful, intentional silence in poetry. "Quietly before evening / our fears / keep becoming," she writes in "Otherwise": "Light scattering in fog."

While the EARLY poems are mostly addressed to a plural or singular "you," and thereby look outwards, or towards an interlocutor, the lyric voice in LATER becomes increasingly inward. "I" and "we" become the primary entities. The themes, too, are more intimate: relationships between two people, the relationship to the self, love, family, sickness, inner life. "What / were we talking about before?" asks one poem, then answers: "Luxurious relics of / melancholy and madness / mark the illusion / of a separation: / metaphor for nearness and Being-Near." These conversations can all be read as conversations with the self. When a "you" appears, it always contains the possibility of another "I." The poems think in spatial metaphors, and are interested in the polarities between inside and out. "By chance we're here, in the same city, / [...] under the same conditions," Schmeidel writes in "Once and For All": "I'm not building a roof for the rest of chance." The inward-looking voice doesn't seal itself off from outside, it includes the social "conditions" in its reflection. Yet the vanishing point of this poetic attention seems to lie "in me," where "the silence / [...] wakes up" ("This Heart").

Speak to me—often the other is only implicitly present. The absence of a concrete "you" transforms into the feeling of absence itself, it stretches into emptiness: "Speak to me / when the coffin of time opens / and I'm unable to die." When loneliness—in which one can still talk to oneself, can still meditate—crosses the threshold to isolation, fear wells up. Existential fear, the fear of death. Is there salvation? In poetry? "I want to be with you all again / before it's too late," the lyric voice assures itself, and us, and poetry in "We Exist": "I want to be there again where / there are questions in people's eyes. [...] // I want to be there again / where the sky touches the horizon / and we go freely next to one another: / silhouettes of our finiteness." These few lines express that we exist not alone, but in plural form ("you all," "people," "we," "our"). They seem to offer hope and a perspective in which "finiteness" can be identified as a sign of our vitality and freedom.

Yet it is often dark in these poems. Autumn, twilight, and "first snowfall in July" ("For Example"). Were we happier when it wasn't so quiet? Or when the word "rebellion" still meant something? The nerves of the "I" in these LATER poems are on edge. Doctors and clinics can only be of limited help. For the "I" is sickened not least of all by society. It is an eerie society of "post-war children" ("Friederike"), where even flower children decorate themselves with "military jackets," and the "fear of barbed wire" threatens in a new way, as if from within ("In Between Word"). "We're living in an emerging ice age," is the dark, prophetic last line of a poem which deals, up to that point, with cancer ("Installation"). In times of cold, undeclared wars, a question begins to flicker: where does conflict actually take place? The possible answers, as in Elisabeth Schmeidel's poems, oscillate between personal, corporeal, and abstract, political symptoms.

Formally, these explorations are very free. Each poem faces anew the task of finding its own form. Here we see an author who knows that there are no certainties to support her—that, ultimately, she can rely on nothing. Nothing but herself—and language, words. In other words: Elisabeth Schmeidel shows us how one writes when one is truly on one's own.

"In the mine field presence," her words dwell on the poetic while scrutinizing the conceptual ("Against"). A daring game played at a great height—"I love the acrobats" ("Lifelong")—in which fall and birth, inspiration and abyss are divided by the blink of an eye. From the mirror of tears that accompanies the free fall, someone sees us—someone who does not let himself be deceived, who loves and mourns for the world, whose eye laughs and cries, like the "clown—escort of my soul" ("My Clown").

4

LATER STILL marks the third section of the poems collected here. Formally, they're yet more multifaceted or heterogeneous than the poems in the other two sections. Long poems and short ones, brief and extended lines, clear stanzas and loosely grouped lines, associative suggestions and narrative sentences. As if something were ending, running out, some would say; I would say rather: as if something were beginning again. "Possible" ends the volume, testing out possible constellations of "yourself," and "death," and "laugh," ending with "died out," which is bookended by "laughed at," and "kept laughing."

Some thematic strains that can be traced through the whole volume but haven't been mentioned here deserve a foreword to themselves. Myths, for example (Troy, the Nibelungen, the Odyssey), or the figure of the child as intractable truth-teller, dream and madness ("Psst, are you crazy! a supervisor grumbles" in "Tra-la-la"), claustrophobia, ("arranged them in glass chests" ["Ad Acta"]), and above all, gender roles, conventions, and relationships between the sexes.

"Excuse Me," for example, presents a lyric "Thinking about. / About love. / About Him. / About my sex." "Only once" does there seem to have been clarity about the speaker's role as "woman"; "I was pregnant, then." A biologic definition. Twice, the poem juxtaposes nine other roles, assumed and claimed, masculine and feminine, including "little Marie / cricket / Sleeping Beauty / mother / daughter / girl." With each repetition, the titular "excuse me" grows more impatient, more pointed. It transforms from apology to challenge, and finally to a command that throws everything into question: "Excuse me. / Or did you know what you do?" The rebelliousness of *Scant Hours* consists in showing us a female voice which autonomously and independently determines, in its every word, when it wishes to speak as a female voice, and when not. And "the feminine" is only one example of a general "Status Quo" of poetic articulation: "A prick into a wasp's nest calls for careful planning."

Of course, what we are reading here is a translation. With incomparable sensitivity and linguistic creativity, Stuart Friebert succeeds not only in bringing Elisabeth Schmeidel's marvelous images and surprising word collages into English; rather, his American English creates a tone that allows the contemporary English-speaking world access to the fine overtones, the voices and moods of Schmeidel's language.

One example must suffice. Take "Schwache Stunden," the German title of a poem in which a voice dives under the frozen surface of a lake, taking an uncanny, romantic journey through secret channels to the sea, where it surfaces somewhere new, only to be found by a fisherman who smashes it against a cliff. Only in the last line does it become clear that the voice comes from a bottle—a poem as message in a bottle. It is a poetic image whose story can also be read as a metaphor for translation: a beautiful and subtle choice for the title.

And what does Stuart Friebert do in English? The English title of "Schwache Stunden" is "Scant Hours." "Weak hours" isn't a standard expression in German; one speaks rather of "a weak moment"—a moment when one is suddenly overcome by fatigue or exhaustion against which the will is powerless. A moment of abandonment when there is no other option, even simply physically. This condition, however, enables an experience that the waking, controlled consciousness normally wouldn't allow. A moment of vulnerability. A moment of expanded perception. A poetic moment. Despite these resonances, "Weak hours," would dramatically miss the mark, as would better or worse variations like frail, light, or faint hours.

"Scant Hours," in contrast, is a surprising, imaginative, and brilliant choice. For luckily, Stuart Friebert is a poet in his own right. "Scant" has Nordic roots, where it means "short" or "brief"; "karg" would be a nice German translation, which carries with it echoes of the English "bare": something open and unprotected. "Barely or scarcely sufficient" is Merriam-Webster's commentary on the adjective "scant." "Oh, if hours only had a hundred minutes," Elisabeth Schmeidel often said in their conversations, Stuart Friebert remembers. The lack of time—in this moment, perhaps in life, in friendship—and the desire to change this, to stretch time. In the now, in writing. In memory. In translation? The slightly extended vowel sounds in "scant" and "hours" subtly convert and transform the alliteration of "sh" sounds in the German title, while the "s" is not lost in English, but appears at the beginning and end, like the walls of an echo chamber. "Scant Hours"—*hearing* the title, a homonym might emerge: "Scanned Hours." Scanned, rhythmical, sung hours. The momentum of poetry.

Translated from German by Anne Posten

THOMAS WILD *teaches German Studies at Bard College. His work focuses on modern and contemporary literature, thought, and cultural history, with special focus on poetry, poetics, and multilingualism. His books include a study of Hannah Arendt's relationships with key postwar German writers, an edition of poetry by Thomas Brasch, and editions of several correspondences of writers and thinkers such as Hannah Arendt, Hilde Domin, Wolfgang Hildesheimer, and Uwe Johnson. Thomas Wild is also co-editor of the upcoming critical edition of* Hannah Arendt's Complete Works.

I EARLY

SEARCHING

Searching for words, for language,
for something and resting inside,
thinking of you
minus the picture of this battle,
this murderous impact
of bodies, I just want to touch
your forehead and breathe
the night sky over the city,
I want to stop glowing, cool down
in the middle of the earth:

morning cools your face.

TOO EARLY

Too early for the evening
belated days
broken hours
in your memory
scars
overgrown spots
potentially
inflammatory hearths

let it remain day today
and between the hours
let things be, cool down
before night comes on.

INSTRUCTIONS

On one day
from below to above
from inside to outside
the sun, rising,
will break through
the skin of the earth and
you'll
talk about it
as usual
give instructions
e.g.
honor old age
fear dear God
don't slurp
and
as usual
you'll
do everything normally
while the ground
under your feet
burns.

OBSERVATION

Entangled
in the wood, an eagle,
pedestal for blackbirds,
busy
ants strangers to him,
the ticking in the timber
the mathematical
formula for leaves.

Do we see him once more
digging into earth's interior
at the sun's feet
mirroring himself
in the water?

Fog soaks
his feathers, frost
kicks in and
leftover motion:
eye in eye
there's still thawing
at noon
it's still
fall.

NIGHT SWALLOWS

Night swallows, rare varieties
splendidly feathered incorruptible
messengers of dark brothers

The wind comes bearing
hidden purposes for you, the father
of a notion of flight
from this palace
edifice become mythos
place of worship of a magical union

The ever stony guest knows
my season, my home
he enters and we are silent.

GEOLOGICAL

Definitely dark.
In spite of that the tracking
dogs follow the streams   lay canals
dry   tear-glazed I relax
memory breaks loudly. Before Catalina.
Cripples trusting their attendants,
elephants washed down. Come on
I can't stand to see blood, you say.
The trail into the canyon's open.
Why so eager?   Protected
comets lie under formations.
Dumping trash forbidden. Indications of
voles   rabies   emeralds.

Volcanoes, overcome by ashes,
and graves full of sun.

DAILY MEMO

Open, record phantoms, remove:
Soul-feathers wet to the bone. Wait!
There's method to the spider's weaving
Cleopatra's image in its spiral. Full museums. Urn-
laws are absent. Rib-fossils in my head. Precise
nuances of adamesque inlays: oxidation according to plan.

In summer the skies remain bright at night.

Decide: free of the stone, the lake's silent.

Glittering uniforms by rails going nowhere.
A buffoon has bartered sex with Daphne:
a gang of guards takes charge of the graves of heroes.

NAVICERT 8

All set:
the sky's intact,
the tree's cut,
night's deep blue.

Footsteps in the net of unknown fishermen,
boats anchor in stone and
ancient animals tussling in rubble.
There was a vineyard here, once upon a time.

Entangled in submarine mines as in roots,
young suns sleep along with their magnificent mother.

OTHERWISE

More often than earlier
your hand reaches into the void and
back comes a fist,
small and hard.

Gods on thrones watch over the flight
of thoughts, time silvers:
slim substitute for illusions in blue.

Long winters. Every year
the surface of the lake freezes,
under fog till noon.
A scrap of blue sky, a step
with you. Quietly, before evening
our fears
keep becoming:
Light scattering in fog.

You're blowing frost flowers, smiling
as if it were the middle of May.

THIS LANDSCAPE

Here you're not allowed to ask
"… and what do you think? … how much longer?"
This landscape is ordained by God like the sea.
Clearly marked, each mountain its form,
each farmer his field. The moor sinks

about six centimeters a year, the change
is slight, borne by the unchanging
eternity of stony fields.
You take a stand against this petrified power
as if it were a matter of winning a victory.

Your cap tight around your ears, you climb
from hollow to hollow across the blanket of snow,
curl up your collar high against the wind.
In town the plows pile the snow to the side,
the Public Works Department
spreads pebbly material on ice-slick roads.

THIS WINTER

This winter illuminates memories.
Counterpose. Dance of flowers, fleeing shadows
and: lisping leaves of trees.

Long torn to pieces, supposed faces,
pictures, taken from the wall years ago,
living eyes in larvae shelved in layers of wax—
phantom images of a world

against which your darkest dream struggles.
The dampness of subterranean passageways
coats your forehead, you long
for the secret: morning fresh as dew,
of the feel of wet grass,
pearls in the calyx of a narcissus.
Blue grapes, hoar-frost subdued
colors replenish those days:
plump and swollen, an expectant
bud of time. Opening itself to the sun.

Shadow-games in the snowy field.
Very small waves roll at you,
in a sea frozen white you hear
no fish, no sound, only yourself,
shielded by the laws of physics:
a shout into the snow smothers itself,
doesn't echo ... doesn't—
a hand cold as your own ...

icy snowballs, in quick succession
missiles big as your fist punch
rasters of holes into the dream
of a childhood fallen from the sky—
it's snowing, snowing!

SCANT HOURS / MOMENTS OF WEAKNESS

Unseen I cross the lake. Above me
the scratching of skates on ice.
The surface holds, I'm sure, dive.
My orientation-sense is dependable.
Soon I reach the Pacific, swim up above,
float on the lightly warmed surface of the water.

Life could be simpler.
Stillness. Have I drowned?
The cork sits fast, no water
in my belly, no wave, no steamer.
Nothing casts me on land.
It won't work without a compromise.
Says my mother. To each his own.
You have to let men be,
close an eye.

Three in the morning. I fall into the net,
am immediately and ungently cast out again.
Frippery, a man says, in our boarding house—
we shape our nightlife.
He polishes anchors.

Warning signs at the coast.
I reach a buoy. Calmly,
used to driftwood it asks:
your message? I blubber, stick
my cork tighter in. Out with it!
the buoy says, more sharply now.
Here we go again, the fisherman complains
and smashes his bottle to bits on the cliff.

OPERATION MOONLIGHT

Scale back
again
evaluate
re-
write
live proportionally
pigment part green
frightened phases
shorten
leveled and
decentralized
thinking.

Two hours of common sense.

Retailer problems.
Confiscated quanta of mind.
Sleep translated
the temporal limit,
stay awake
devaluate
live.

ONE LAST TIME

Set loose your anchors from this house
now and not a day later.

For the last time doves
cry over the breakers, hunt
fish back to the sea.

One last time they hurry
across the footbridge to land, listen
to the sirens in the fog.

Too late for silent sorrow

from the coral forests flames lash out
scorch words against the wind.

CARRY ME OUT

Let the many-thousand-year Reich
arise anew and forget me
forever and always and
never again
not even just once
or
don't let this planet
be older than
the day (which I forgot)

he she it you
and me there

go back
out of the words out
of hate hunger strange—and loneliness
out of this time
coated with the sweat
of fear
out of alien
power alien
might the alien
past alien
future
carry me out
let me die elsewhere.

II LATER

FREQUENCIES

Being able to begin
there
where your voice
lingers—
frequencies
hidden like animals
in woods, which become
alive
at night
with shadows of fallen
angels, with strange commands.
Being able to keep going
in your voice.

LUXURIOUS RELICS

What
were we talking about before?
Where
has it led us
when unrecognized
we walked toward then past
each other, as an apparently harmless
wind blew your silhouette into the net
of my time through which my body
coils?
Luxurious relics of
melancholy and madness
mark the illusion
of a separation:
metaphor for nearness and Being-Near.

ONCE AND FOR ALL

Let's hope we're here by chance.
Paint chance a faithful face,
remain friendly, attribute injustice
to no one, not ourselves either, in the end
the tobacconist knows my brand, there's
a shoemaker here and bread in the stores.

Pleasantly here by chance. Responsible.
I just can't do anything but appear conscientious.
Once again we make signs behind us, read timetables,
which just happen to amount to a system i.e.,
you shake your locks, take your seat.
By chance others take the same train.

By chance we're here, in the same city,
the same concert, under the same conditions.
I'm not building a roof for the rest of chance.
When it gets later than I hope,
I've for once ignored the time. Nothing more.

THIS HEART

this wingless affliction
this persistent roaring of the sea
in this 1000-year stone
this stone
this fossil
once there was rain here
and this rain
this agitating against
the wind, this wind
whose storming power
this heart deeply
driven into the earth,
this quaking center
the shining
this wing-bearing blue
and you
very near
when the silence
finally
wakes up
in me.

SHADOW DAYS

for sleeplessly tormented
love
in which I want to believe
without contradiction
without condition
without caution.

Parades
of the Golden West,
of victorious armies,
of power
of the banal
of hoaxed hope
of Daily Bread and Hereafter.
Parades
to the cross
of nailed
starved
children.

Shadows
grown sleepless
like me
populate
memory.

AGAINST

this my sun in
this my winter and
against the shadows of ob-
jects
shouldn't this wall
be opposite me
so I could beat against it?

Against the light. Winters. Longer
rays and cooler than—.
Pale-greens at the window.
Each scant ray brings
unrest, shadows, darkly clear
against surfaces, beset by
the grip of matter:
in the opposing light.

—

I am Pharaoh—or
Greek. In any case:
marble. Caryatidic
smiles: yet another millennium,
yet another attempt, once again
upriver. Stone for stone.

—

Gray moths, no dream escapes.
Not until morning: wings of sun in the east.

Flamingos, bickering and pink.
Moment of remembrance,
in the mine field presence:
sleep-baby-sleep.

WE EXIST

I want to be there again where
there are questions in people's eyes.
I want to be then again when beauty
and joy are sensed among tears.
I want to be with you all again
before it's too late.

My tranquil valley here remains a hope
of being buried in the cemetery in line
with tradition (left of the road).
A peaked cross to say farewell,
a bouquet of dandelions for the future.
One last time
the hope they might rise up
without cliffs at their back, and my smile
striking the granite of their eyes again.

I want to be there again
where the sky touches the horizon
and we go freely next to one another:
silhouettes of our finiteness.

ANSWER ME

When voices still invaded
the stillness and chorai,
colorfully garbed,
showed the way,
when wind going mad
still frightened us,
when night
still protected day and
beat with the same heart,
were we happier?
when rain and snow
sea and stone
sun and tomorrow
lily and light
stood as signs of rebellion
a priori for
the present?

FOR EXAMPLE

Something happens. Something or other.
Perhaps for the 6th or 7th time or
however many times.
Up to this first time for you.
You startle.
Landing from nowhere.

You pointing e.g.
a leaf's falling! bewilders them.
Leaves fall. Why the pointer?
Calm down.
Many leaves fall in the fall.
It's May.
First snowfall in July,
grapes on Christmas trees,
no cause for excitement,
you've had nervous breakdowns before:
they treat you, carefully, distribute
jobs unobtrusively (they believe).

Fall's nearing. You're almost restored.
Look, all the leaves are falling!
You nod your head.
The men lay an arm around your shoulder,
the women say: that has to be done!
and sweep leaves from the balconies.

Someone points: a leaf's falling!
You all stand still, look at the falling leaf.
He pulls you along:
in fall many leaves fall.
You nod.

INSTALLATION

The earliest decades did not pass over
my chest without a trace. Knife pleats, cross striped,
recall the thoroughness of a radiologist,
who mammogrammed me once.
Twenty-five percent of all cases, he says, can,
I emphasize (and he emphasizes) CAN become malicious.

When I met one of my siblings
years later, he cried out, horrified:
Where are your delightful little boobs!
I was holding my child in my arms.
Ever since we don't talk about it.

Times change or tempora mutantur, writes
a great aunt from Africa. Because of modesty, and
she persists, it was high time to put a corset
on my daughter.

I add vanilla to the banana-milk, continue the past-
perfect enlightenment campaign about dessert. Look,
I say, today I'm using body-folds as a muff ...
We're living in an emerging ice age.

CHIRPING

Again I find myself at the window, again with a view
outside, cigarette, coffee, one arm embracing the other,
out over the curtain, which only covers the bottom half
of the window, with a view, as I said, outside.
On occasion the house is being watched.

Of course I'm looking for nothing, no domestic animal
that's run off or a forgotten toy, just looking quite
openly and as usual, the entrance to my eyes converting
the sources of light. On account of the brightness—yet
again I run short of enlightenment, wash dishes,
pack up books and whatever I don't intend to read
in the next months, put out milk for the family.

PREVENTIVELY DEFINED

Gradual decay. Romanticism by the milligram.
Along old walls, in branches of gnarled trees,
a bird's nest. Nonsense, good, your father doesn't know!

They lock the door, want to be alone.
The grandmother assumes command. On the one hand,
she finds it embarrassing, on the other, she says, I mean
other hand, life's like that. I know.
Relieved, grandmother goes on talking.
Do you understand? she finally asks. Yes,
I reply, without a rooster no hens.
This simile doesn't seem risky.
I can calm her, more I don't know.

He's monsignor and fat,
his passion's teaching religion,
he raises his finger (several
rings on his hand), examines, at the blackboard: marriage.

Because I basically see familiar issues re henhouses,
I'm silent, have to sit down: a black mark for
minimal co-work.

I like being with the chickens, in the henhouse, collect freshly
laid eggs early in the morning and once a month clean
the ladder.

SOMETHING'S UP

Today there's nothing much going on.
Often there's nothing much going on.
Often nothing's going on.
Mostly everything just stays the same.

I close the blinds: because of the view.
For a year now: green hills.
Wrong: in winter, gray, brown, white
hills. Nevertheless.
There are hills and hills.
These hills are such hills.
Day out   day in   year out   year in.
Nothing you can do about it. They won't turn
hillier or more or less.
After looking away, when you look again:
everything's the same.
The hills. The hill. A hill
seldom appears alone. Dayoutyearin.
Are they staring at me or I at them?
No two ways about it: they're staring.
I can prove it: the blinds are open.
Green hills, at the next window, the next
house, the next corner, the next year.

To be safe I'm getting curtains, too.

TO PLEASE YOU

To please you I cut my hair.
So that mistakes would occur more seldom.
My ears stand way out.

At twenty we innocently ate pearl barley.
The neighbor's dog arrived in December.
The cockchafer couple overwintered in the gum tree.
We moved to the country, two years later.
The carrier pigeons took birthday wishes,
otherwise no news.
Christmas the troubles began.
Frozen to death the swallows fell from the roof:
they missed migration. For the feast:
pancakes with cottage cheese and illuminated
gum tree (as last year). Suddenly
you want turkey and spruce. I'm writing
your mother about the pregnancy.
The postcard signed by her says:
a splendid year for common adders.
Even the neighbor's dog's in denial.
The carrier pigeons squat under the gutter.
No birthday wish, apparently.
You take a pigeon, promise not
to stay away more than forty years.

Two hours later: you come,
with short hair, ears sticking out.
Cowards, the neighbor's dog yaps.
Stork tales, the pigeons coo and,
that's what you get, neighbor.

FRIEDERIKE

Memories of China. Women's shoes not larger than
a child's hand. Monstrous, says an uncle. Later they
explain he's my brother. Second-hand, by other marriages.
Our family history's branched out. Migrant stork.

Nights it's dark. I shouldn't cry so.
The nun at the convent wants to be nice, runs a hand
again and again over my head. She herself's without family.
One has to feel sorry for half-orphans too. Was she called Antonia?

Sundays braided bread. A slice for everyone. My friend's
called Friederike and eats the second one up by herself. One won't
invite her again, daughter of divorced parents,
from a good home originally, one can see where that leads.
Post-war children, common property to all, no braided bread
on Sunday. Fancy cakes only on birthdays. People are getting
on and never again saveyourselfwhoevercan …

Her mother's silent. A complicated (long?) story.
Reconstruction and men. Growing up is the future, what
else. Come, let's go to the grave at the cemetery.

Friederike and I want to go to the movies.
She's also got a brother, second-hand, to whom she's become
an aunt. People talk of economic miracle and Sunday ham,
they're just not right with my going around with Friederike. Really
not. Because of her strong-arming and in view of the future.
And because of the braided bread, one slice per head.

LIFELONG

I love the acrobats,
run to the circus at every opportunity.
The first headstand almost broke my neck.
My mother entered our sunny rooms.
Each birth with the head in front!
(I still cried then.)

She's standing in the door, labor pains set in:
Legs on the floor, she orders,
have I given birth to a clown?
Fifteen years, I scoff,
issue the birth certificate.

As expected the woman begins to cry.
A man rushes to us. Going down
I land on my soles.
Step by step
past her and the man
and on beyond
with my head in front with my head …

MY CLOWN

The clown—escort of my soul
doesn't let himself be deceived:
when it laughs he cries and vice versa.
He knows what it's a matter of
in love as well.

My clown loves himself and the world,
therefore he's often in mourning—
about the love in his world.
The soul grows quiet too, whenever
love wanders over the graves
pale as a shadow.

Many have meant love to us,
almost beaten my clown to death—
if my soul hadn't lent him wings …
but he escaped,
and not just once.

IN BETWEEN WORD

I'm looking for a word between inter and national,
know my way around neither here nor there,
pick since I was a child barbs from wires,
plunge once a day from the mast onto the flag.

My daughter forgives me:
in the eyes of the moralists
I die
miserably
and begin
in Ancient Egypt.
Tut-ench-Amon's the mayor,
Alexander the Great as interceptor.
Now we're a step along,
no Cup without hard work.
With a leader's quality.

You comfort me this time too.
Someone more important—Walter H.—says his words
would be heard differently here than where you are.

And further. In a military jacket, veiled, decorated,
right or left … March, whatever.
Some pound the table right away.
What's missing, they say, is sadism, a healthy portion.
Harikari? I decline.
You know my fear of barbed wire,
make an issue of it.

IMMOVABLES

Everything about knots and braiding ropes.
Listen for the creek, dive into the lake,
because of the truth, reasonable that is.
The season, a nomadic woman. Assuming
the case I wandered in spring
around the Earth.

Are you sad? Finally lonely?
Even your pulse chokes in a vacuum.
Does anyone here know any better?
Pericles was bewitching, the sailor laughs.
Of course I envy him, in Greek.

I go along with the army, my lemmings,
up to the coffer dam. Quickly turn
off. Only in the afterworld
does death show up suddenly.
Thessaloniki is far away.

FOUND OBJECTS

It doesn't help that your spores shine,
your hand's bigger than mine, your house
looks out through four-by-eight windows.
The silence is deceptive, muzzles
the moon without regard to sex.

Spaghetti al dente. Your favorite dish.
Moths in the red wine. Alarm. The little fireflies
are stirring. Morse-light to the moon:
Airship with calf on the way.

Your house is in Troy. Civil defense—
number 230, you say, chewing basil.
No problem, a firefly flashes,
we're analphabets.

MARCHFOUR

clouds pour from my eyes
cloak the sun—
what's become of my tears?

SPEAK TO ME

I seize this hour
in gold
into the morning
and give you—

a mouth of sun
under a day still fallow,
fish
still in the waters—
how deep the silence is!

Princes, said to be dead, light their fire
and between the flaming cities
in this archaic land:
foreign peoples in nothingness, black as fire.

Speak to me
when the coffin of time opens
and I'm unable to die.

III LATER STILL

MY SOUL

My soul sheds feathers
perhaps it was once more many-colored
perhaps even skittish
with soft down and strong
wings, my soul—
a buzzard, a chick, a Lohengrin.

In its raw state
way past midnight
scanty gestures
musical scales
oceanics.

In my bed there's a faun
with my soul, the faithless one.

GAMBIT

And our fathers
demand redemption,
no misgivings
breath breaks forth
from deep tunnels.
When they abandoned us
we shook
the men awake
searched
in the dreams
of daughters, screamed
at the rain
our branchia filled with water.
Soprano, Gregorian.

Down to the roots of rivers
refuse leaked out of our houses
and mud suffocated the mussels.

The prize for
the doll of the queen,
dark things
in the eyes of the fathers,
for snake and Abel,
ask your abbess,
we're the prize.

WHATEVER'S THE MATTER WITH YOU

Even in the darkest darkness no attempt goes unnoticed.
The criticism of observers follows in the wake of.
You want everything all at once, they say, take your time.
And that to me! While with every imaginable trick I strive
to make up for what melted away between my fingers
like wax on the wings of Icarus.

Report from the radio:
Hairline tears in the wings of airplanes.

Lame from fear for days.
Whatever's the matter with you, my mother writes,
every hour a sparrow falls out of its nest.

EXCUSE ME

Thinking about.
About love.
About Him.
About my sex.

I was a woman only once:
I was pregnant, then.

Excuse me, you
knights
generals
clowns
grasshoppers
ambassadors
fathers
sons
boys
brothers.
Excuse me, friends,
I was myself
only once
then
and I was pregnant.
Excuse me,
that before and after
I was nothing but
a knight's maiden
generals' staff widow
little Marie
cricket
Sleeping Beauty

mother
daughter
girl
sister.
Excuse me.
Or did you know what you do?

FROM THE PROGRAM

My room has no window, a double folding door instead.
In front of it grating belly-high. Balcony, in French.

People like me do not leap off. We talk about it, pretend
to understand those who leap and/or hang themselves. A lie.

We have the other way out: when there's nothing else—then
hope. Pale ghost in the heart. Both wings of the double-
folding door close, down the steps you go, out past
the gate. Most obedient servant of society.

Men in uniform (in some cases women):
the mechanic, mailman, delivery man, the refuse guy (no
woman), the plumber (also no woman, see mechanic),
gym teacher, ski instructor, doctor, the nurses (staffed
as caretakers by men), the secretary (writing desk too),
convent nuns (living separately).

In the name of the Law, you are arrested!
Finally.
Swindled, Mr. Lurk laughs and tips his cap.
Splendid, I say and, have a nice weekend.

STATUS QUO

Import/Export. Problems. Butter, extension cords and
a surplus of umbilical cords and sockets already overcrowded.
The computer remains stubborn: Adam and Eve. No Ifs
and Buts. Crisis in rib bone and tool culture.

Maintain a rigid bearing throughout life. You may pinch fresh
vegetables. Household goods are increasing, she's finally sensible
and he's winning tournaments, the third remodeling, climacteric periods
and what comes with them (he thinks). Let's see your little legs.

The official adviser in women's issues dispenses with
roses, for professional reasons, too many thorns. Operation
Evergreen. Supervision of back gardens. Rationing of
kinds of bread and lists with probability index:
old woman S. at the top
then the divorced, with or without child
then unmarrieds over twenty-five
then those in a turbulent marriage,
last rubric: various.

A prick into a wasp's nest calls for careful planning:
we're laboring behind a closed window. Beekeeper garb
re size and a reserve helmet for the Under-Secretary of State,
female sex.

TRA-LA-LA

In the express letter of the summer before last
the invitation had come to me
to join the Ring of the Nibelungs.
Very cordially. Your President. Signature.

I read sender and address, knock at the neighbor's.
Nobody there. Not on the other side either.
Finally, I ring my bell,
open up, lay the invitation in a drawer.

My drawers are unlocked, the invitation's
been gone for some time. The President's waiting.
Three violets to the polling place. For Siegfried.
Psst, are you crazy! a supervisor grumbles,
this election stays secret. He points to the ballot boxes.

Hang it all! I shout, where's the President around here?
The hallway guards arrive, take me away in orderly fashion.
The right corner of my mouth sags down lower.
Tra-la-la … a … tra-la-laa … la … la.

AD ACTA

As a boy he'd collected stones, marked them and
arranged them in glass chests. If dust had for all that
pressed through the cracks, he'd loosened the glasses
from their frames, carefully, and polished the amethyst,
which stood at the start of the collection.

The library, he says, you can find everything here.
Under the desk, the wooden case, locked
with metal clasps and nails: uranium.
Nothing's lacking.
An amulet from Tibet.
Protection against spirits.

She finds herself in drawer 325.
Memorandum 10.001.
Lying on her back, with both feet against
the drawer overhead, hands braced sideways
against the chest's walls, pushes herself, as small
as possible, forward, her head turned to the opening.
Word by word. Shove by shove.
As soon as the crack allows, she slips outside,
opens a window. There's a draft, he shivers.
She opens. A gust of air whirls through the table
of contents. The key words! he cries and wildly
clutches at the inventory fluttering around.
Hey you, I say, the wind in my face does me good.

MIMIC

The backdrop of the (green) trees pushes forward,
she climbs into the boughs. He says:
one can lower the glass partition.
Not necessary, she says.

In the fireplace, withering marguerites.
Plastic flowers in the corner: America,
he says. Lives, she says.
Illusion of eternity, he says.

Gleaming red of tree trunks.
Back into the arm chair.
He pours wine out, they move
toward each other, don't hurt themselves.
Sudden turn. In profile
she glides past him and the question

why is she here …

The plantain, he says, the bright spot.
She takes the seat he offers.
Sun towards evening, up above, clear view.
One can lower the glass partition,
he says. She says: not necessary.
With the push of a button, if it blinds you,
he said.

SCREAMING

When I scream I have to say why.
Other people don't scream much anymore.
I mean, just look at them. Men look and stop.

Today I could have said: Listen, the voice
going in's too full. Try saying that to someone,
he'll make you analyze it, he'll make you analyze it.
I start thinking influence. Otherwise I'd go to pieces.

You see, he'd say. I'd say things he wants to hear.
We'd go on talking, and he'd be nice enough to say
things I want to hear. Mr.—but I'm screaming now.
So hard there are little blue knots on my neck.
Take it easy, the man says, easy. And the sun stops
at the window. No, I scream. My husband isn't
just an architect, he's a gardener, too.

Then there was the year he studied soils—
plants need sun and water. No sun today so he
tries water. Water plants, he says. I'm so
leached out we go to lunch. Notice how careful
he is to have enough water on the table.

I'm touched. Slowly, I think. Please, slowly.
Lean forward, bump my head. A woman
150 years old says, Be Noah. Scream.

IT'S VERY SIMPLE

I can't think when I cry, I just cry.
You're quieter afterwards, there's
a bridge and water underneath, gambled
away you might say. If you're there,
you can watch the birds picking
little crabs from the sand.

Once there was a man talking to a child
on the bridge: That's life, he said, stuck
out an arm toward the last bit of sun,
the child said, Yes, and the man gave
the child a folder from an airline.
The child said, I like you a lot,
the man waved.

You go through the whole alphabet,
but you can't think of people like that.
Oh, sometimes friends call or even stop by,
Don't cry, they say. Please, not when we're here.

Their wives are crying at home. I'm sorry,
but they are. The men always have some explanation.
It's water and earth, I say. I'm whispering now,
it's about love. Suddenly they run off.   Bye.

WHAT THEY SAID TO THE CHILD

The child wished they'd go away,
the daily visitors, uncles, aunts,
with their bowed heads. Milk chocolates.
And. No second summer will follow, no one
can lie from one to the next summer gaunt in bed
one summer long and then one more.
No, that's no summer, dearie.

The way to the bed is endless.
Flowers on the table. The child
at the window wants to wave, suppresses
a move, runs from the room,
down the stairs,
onto the gravel and
into the shade of the lime tree.

They lift the man from the car,
carry him upstairs.
You wait here, they say to the child.

A REQUEST

Do look, my daughter says,
you can swim in the lake, go for
a row, surf, skate on the ice, cross
the lake with the ferry, or with
long-distance skis ... fly across the lake.

And I'm ashamed:
back of the listing of available qualities
there's a request.

MANY-COLORED EYES

Telefants crouch, satiated
behind my bed
gobble up
all the children
I'm dreaming
chafers   fly away

CHILDREN'S THRILLER

The princess is bald, the magic lamp broken,
the boy on the dolphin a statue.

When Anna wets the bed he'll come for sure and if
he doesn't come, because he's so big and black so
he gets stuck in the keyhole, then father will come,
because Anna's wet her bed.
Anna is four.
For the princess a wig, please.
Take off your pants so I can hit you better.

In reality he's a human being, they say, with a heart.
When Anna sits on his lap nothing happens.
One must talk with the woman. Fewer antics, more
Anna instead. She's always trustworthy and pocketless.

Anna wakes up, hears him scream, crawls under
the covers. Aladdin, she whispers, get him stuck,
close the keyhole!

AUSTRALIA

Didn't you say you're going to Australia?
Politics here causes fear and anxiety.
We page around in the atlas daily. Australia.

How do you get to Australia?
Doesn't matter.
What do they do there?
Also doesn't matter.
Life grows harder and harder.
I speak German,

that's not enough. Our child's growing up
and isn't for Canada. Too northerly,
she thinks. I could convince her, Australia,
and a landscape in sight, which
takes our breath away. Not spectacular, no, not exactly.

THE STONY SEA

—Where do you want to go?
—I don't know.
—When will you come back?
—Soon. I'm telling you: soon.
—Why don't you tell me where you're going?
—I don't know. I'll return.
—You do that often now.
  Why don't you take me along?
—I have to be alone.
—Should I move out?
—I'm not going away from you.
  I want to be with myself.
—If something happens to you?

I bend over her, straighten the bedspread.
Dark metal. Moon-white mirrors. Some snow on
the south slope. Nightclub for clever foxes at woods' edge.
Gathering of stars in the midst of mountain peaks. Matte,
elevated hills, curves. Downward. Overtaking forbidden.

Additionally: the sea pounds roots, petrified wings, black &
blue at the edge of the basin. Stone after stone, a night
sinks, cold as the left ventricle.

—I heard you, you're still in the stairwell.
—Nothing's happened, do you believe me now?
—Was it nice?
—It did me good. Brief enough for you?
—35 minutes. I almost fell asleep.
   The moon gives off a lot of light, please open the window,
   I can breathe fresher then.
—Did you pack my schoolbag for tomorrow?
—Yes. ... Next time, will you take me along?

DON'T SHOOT

at stars
children and tin cans
don't shoot at all

it's always about what's beyond the target,
beyond life
right into the kingdom of the dead
body by body

slashed violated murdered
there's screaming
growing weaker
grown silent
comes back
soul by soul
there's silence
in holy fury,

the heart's hushed
hope for change.

WHERE

Are you pouring time out to, when
the hourglass plugs up and
forests lie rooted out in the riverbed?

Whom are you giving the handful of dust?
How many chickens do you consume daily?

That's what the bird of passage dies of.

WORDS

Words hem fragments of the night
morning puts off coming on
drunk on sleep I fumble
for a breather
for equatorial grammar
for the bolster
for my aching neck

my old storyteller keeps to the shadows
at daybreak he puts out
the word and the light.

FARTHER

I want to get farther away from you all
want to sheathe myself
in sharp-edged grasses
cover myself with many
many ...
blossoms of larkspur

When the silvery moon cries
it's time.

POSSIBLE

to laugh yourself to death
laugh at yourself
laugh to yourself
laugh having laughed
having laughed to
having laughed at
died out kept laughing.

REMEMBERING HER

When we landed in Amsterdam the summer of 1962—the group of Oberlin college students enrolled in our German Department's summer program it was my turn to direct—"Bettina"* Schmeidel welcomed us onto the tour bus, in which she and the driver would ferry us back to Vienna, the site of the session.

An art student at the Akademie der Bildenden Künste at the time, she'd been engaged to serve as my assistant, to whom I turned again and again, given her intelligence and worldly-wise savvy, for help with issues far beyond the usual scope of arranging overnights on the journey back to Vienna, answering all manner of students' questions, and being generally available in emergencies.

Karl Krolow, in Darmstadt, was our first stop on the way to Vienna before we motored on to visit Ilse Aichinger and her husband Günter Eich at their home in Bad Reichenhall. Among others, their poems had moved me so deeply I felt compelled to

---

*   Pia reports that "Bettina", as many of us knew her, would have wanted to return to her baptized name on any documents at the end of her life. Though her parents admired the writer Bettina von Arnim and wanted to name their daughter after her, no saint was called "Bettina," so given the law at the time they decided on "Elisabeth" instead. Incidentally, one other surname she used was "Grubbauer," for having been briefly married to the architect Peter Grubbauer; and "Behn" yet another, which she adopted when "coming out" as a poet in the 70s, chosen for admiration of Aphra Behn, a writer like Bettina in a "world of men." Aphra was also a "spy," and I suspect Bettina thought of herself as one at times too, for having crept up on humans, especially "innocent" children in particular, before slipping away to mull what she'd witnessed.

translate; and they graciously consented to host us for a reading from their work. When Krolow entertained questions after his reading, Bettina's were so searching it was obvious she was writing poems as well. By and by, I learned she was also writing poems in English; but it would be a while, given her extreme modesty, before I could coax some out of her, which then led to an ongoing exchange of poems. Soon I couldn't help translating her German poems; and when, among others, notable journals like *Field* and *Malahat Review* snapped some up, I urged her to start thinking of collecting them, joking she could even, artist that she was, design the eventual cover.

In the 70s, visiting Bettina and her daughter Pia in Zell am See while I was on a tour with one of my books, Bettina and I finally put together a collection of her poems, in which I managed to interest a German publisher. Alas, something must have gone wrong between them, and the manuscript was never published. To make matters perhaps "worse," when Bettina accompanied me to Salzburg, where Ilse Aichinger had invited me to read with her at the Traklhaus/Leselampe, and I showed Ilse some of Bettina's poems, Ilse said to Bettina: "You're likely the best unknown poet writing in German." At that point, I kept after Bettina to send the manuscript around, but for unknown reasons—perhaps she never did so?—it never found a publisher. Aside from an occasional exchange of notes, we drifted apart till I learned early this century she was in the throes of a serious illness, and more silence set in ...

When I learned of Bettina's death in 2012, at the age of 67, I began a correspondence with Pia, with the urge to see what Bettina might have left by way of her poems, and a plea to see if I might make a book of them. When Pia wrote that Bettina had left "a suitcase" of "papers" and sent me some 100+ texts, some in Bettina's handwriting, I was ecstatic! Putting everything aside, I set about feverishly ferrying the most intact, in some cases most legible, into my brand of "smooth" English. With Pia's blessing, who with her own good eye and ear, not to forget her intimate knowledge of her mother's words and ways, vetted my versions and made valuable suggestions, we were able to build twin collections: the German originals I sent to Matthias Klein and Christiane Wyrwa at scaneg Verlag/Munich. If Bettina only knew that they are publishing them right now! And Pinyon Publishing in Montrose, Colorado is publishing the English translations about the same time. If only …

As the reader will discern, many of the poems sail into the dangerous waters of illness, anger, and despair. We had many a conversation about the eroding political landscape of her beloved Austria. She'd order another "langen braunen" (her go-to Austrian pick-me-up), light another cigarette I'd smuggle her in some quantities, and start sketching and scribbling away on café tablecloths …

—Stuart Friebert